Pick Me Up!

Fun Songs for Learning ASL Signs!

SIGN2ME

Created by Sign2Me the developers of world's first ASL Baby Sign Language program, SIGN *with your* BABY®.

Acknowledgements

Music Composed, Arranged & Produced By: Roger Treece
Lyrics By: Nancy Stewart, Roger Treece, Robert Berg, Bob Tarcea, Dr. Joseph Garcia
Recorded & Mixed By: Roger Treece at The Living Room Studios, Kirkland, Washington with additional recording by Steve Culp at Triad Studios, Redmond, Washington and John Morton at Crooked Box, Federal Way, Washington.
Vocals (alphabetical): Sandra Anderson, Steve Bolanos, Thea Renee Cole, Carl Connor-Kelly, Missi Hale, Dave Irish, Brandon Katz, Lauren Kinhan, Kelly Kunz, H.B. Radke, Aimee Salomon, Roger Treece, Libby Torrance.
Background Voices: Bobby Tarcea, jr., Brian Tarcea
Midi Programming: Roger Treece
Keyboards & Piano: Roger Treece
Guitar: John Morton
Double Bass: Doug Miller
Drums: Ben Smith
Sax & Flute: John Goforth
Trumpet: Brad Allison

Cover Design & Guidebook Layout: Gaelan Kelly
Cartoon Illustrations: Casey McGahan
Additional Illustrations: Shawn Diaz, Alexander Eckardt, Dan Engler, Kristine Svehla-Brown
Written By: Robert Berg, Dr. Joseph Garcia, Judith Anderson-Wright, with contributions from Linda Easton-Waller
Edited By: Bob Tarcea, Lee Strucker
Proofread By: Judith Anderson-Wright, Alexander Eckardt, Dan Engler, Bernadette Stanek, Donald Stone, Stacia Neil, Brian Tarcea, Angel Cook, Melissa "echo" Greenlee
Sign Illustration Concept Design: Harry (Hawk) Jones
Illustrations: Lee Shapiro, Alexander Eckardt, Shawn Diaz, Robert Berg
Sign Sequence & Activity Design: Dr. Joseph Garcia, Nancy Stewart, Robert Berg, Bob Tarcea, Kelly Kirchmar
Evaluation Coordinator: Judith Anderson-Wright

Photography: Bethanie Brown, Monta Briant, Alexander Eckardt, Stan McMeeken, Kristine Svehla-Brown, Bob Tarcea, Chris Smith

Video Sequences Executive Producer: Bob Tarcea
Video Sequences Written, Produced, & Directed By: Robert Berg
Multimedia Design & Production: Alexander Eckardt
Videography: Stan McMeeken, Alexander Eckardt
Video & Audio Editing: Alexander Eckardt
Narrator: Melanie Workhoven
CD Art Design: Kristine Svehla-Brown, Alexander Eckardt
Illustrations By: Shawn Diaz, Alexander Eckardt, Casey McGahan, Kristine Svehla-Brown
Teacher: Nickie Gael
Signing Students (alphabetical): C. Riley Brown, Matthew Brown, Isaiah Cormier, Savannah Cormier, Emma Hall, Nicholas Hunter, Livia Kong, Dylan Koski
"Brand New Day" Demonstration: Joseph Garcia
Make-up: Omi
Digital Photography: Bob Tarcea, Chris Smith, Alexander Eckardt
Child Coordinator: Judith Anderson-Wright
Set Decoration: Kristine Svehla-Brown

Contents

Page 6

Page 10

Page 16

Page 58

Page 60

Contents

Introduction

Why are songs like "The Itsy Bitsy Spider" and "Wheels on the Bus" so popular among young children? One reason is that children can use their hands to participate in these songs even before they can sing them… And using hand gestures is fun! Participating in a song by using body movement also helps reinforce the meaning of the lyrics.

Studies show that combining music and movement is a powerful tool for language learning. However, this tool is often under-utilized. That's because most song activities use gestures that have no application outside the context, or story, of the songs. What if instead, songs were created with hand movements that could be used by pre-verbal babies outside of the song activities to help them clearly express their thoughts and needs? What if Pre-K students and six to 10 year olds could use these movements as the foundation for learning a second language? Now they can… Enter "Li'L Pick Me Up!"

The development team at Sign2Me carefully produced this CD and Guidebook, fine-tuning and testing extensively in 25 childcare centers from around the US, so children, parents, caregivers and teachers could take full advantage of the powerful learning that comes from combining music and signs. We chose American Sign Language (ASL) signs so they could be used in many different contexts and settings. ASL is the third most-used language in the United States and offers a rich vocabulary of simple signs that are widely used and recognized throughout the US and Canada.

Today, "Pick Me Up!" is used with all age groups, from babies to high school and University-level ASL classes. "Pick Me Up!" makes learning ASL vocabulary simple and fun for everyone! "Li'L Pick Me Up!" makes it fun to learn over 200 ASL signs that are useful to almost all children, and adults as well. Songs like "Brand New Day" will help babies learn to identify and label familiar daily activities. "Please Change My

Diaper" will help toddlers develop an awareness of bodily functions and empower them to let their parents and caregivers know when it's time for a change. Preschoolers can learn to identify a variety of foods in "Sometimes When I'm Hungry." And children of all ages can use the animal signs they will learn in "There's a Tiger Walking" and "Go to the Zoo."

By introducing ASL signs to young children, you are giving them a foundation for a second language, a precious gift they can continue to use for the rest of their lives. Moreover, compelling research indicates that using ASL signs simultaneously with spoken English can significantly improve the signer's English literacy skills.

"Li'L Pick Me Up!" Takes advantage of this new discovery while it brings great fun and entertainment to everyone who participates. So… *Let's get started!*

Pre-K, Isaiah, signs his love for airplanes.

Enhanced CD Bonus Material

The bonus material supplied on your "Li'L Pick Me Up!" Enhanced CD has been designed to simplify and enhance the learning and leading of Sign2Me® activities and to offer you a fun bonus song. The bonus material is not essential for the successful use of this product. Although the "Li'L Pick Me Up!" Enhanced CD will work with most Mac and PC computer platforms some CD or DVD-ROM drives will not access the Enhanced CD material. Placing our Enhanced CD in your Mac or PC computer CD-ROM Drive will not hurt the drive or the CD if your drive or system is incompatible. You simply will not be able to access the bonus material.

Start by placing your "Li'L Pick Me Up!" CD into a CD or DVD drive in your computer and wait several seconds. This should automatically launch the "Pick Me Up!" Bonus Material main menu listing the following items:

Multimedia Options

1. How to Learn an Activity

2. How to Lead an Activity

3. "Brand New Day" Demonstrated by Dr. Joseph Garcia

4. Bonus Song "More..."
   • How to Use This Bonus Song
   • Listen to "More..."

5. SIGN *with your* BABY® Product Overview

6. Reminder Series Product Overview

7. Instructors' Network Overview

On-line Resources

8. "Pick Me Up!" On-line

9. What's New at Sign2Me

10. Feedback

By placing the "Li'L Pick Me Up!" CD in your computer you will automatically launch the bonus material menu.

Items 1 through 7 (above) access content that resides on your "Li'L Pick Me Up!" Enhanced CD.
Items 8 through 10 will automatically link you to our Sign2Me Web site if your computer has an active Internet connection.

Troubleshooting

If the "Pick Me Up! Bonus Material" screen does not launch automatically, open the file entitled "Start" which you will find listed in the root directory of the CD. If you are unable to access this and other CD files from your computer, your CD-ROM drive or computer operating system may be incompatible with Enhanced CD's.

Disclaimer: Sign2Me® makes no warranty of any kind regarding the compatibility of the "Li'L Pick Me Up!" Enhanced CD with any computer system. For answers to frequently asked troubleshooting questions, please go to our "Li'L Pick Me Up!" Troubleshooting page on our Web site at :
www.sign2me.com/shop/product70.html

Software Requirements

Video Segments – Require Windows Media Player for PC or Quicktime for Macintosh. These come free with their respective operating systems and can be updated for free at www.microsoft.com and www.apple.com.

Bonus Song – Playable from any audio software that supports MP3 files. To play it in a Music CD player, you must first write the track to a separate music CD using your computer's CD writing software and hardware. (See "Bonus Song" below.)

Pick Me Up! On-line, What's New, Feedback, and Credits – Require an Internet connection and a Web browser. Place the enhanced CD into your computer CD or DVD drive and click on the menu item of your choice.

Bonus Song

The bonus song, "More..." is the same song as "More Milk", only the vocals are silent where you would normally sing the food or drink, so you can sing and sign your own favorite items (i.e. more water, more carrots). You can hear this song by clicking on "More…" From the "Pick Me Up!" Bonus Song menu.

To play this song in a Music CD player, you must first write the song file to a new, blank CD. To do this, you must have an Enhanced CD-compatible source drive and a CD writer in your computer. Use the "More" file (MP3 format) found in the Bonus Song folder on the Enhanced CD as your source file. Then follow the instructions in the manuals for your CD Writer or CD writing software for creating an "Audio CD." An activity plan for this song is provided on page 56-57.

How to Use This Activity Guidebook

Fun Songs for Learning ASL Signs

To facilitate the learning and leading of activities, we use color-coding as a means of organizing and clarifying information in this guidebook. Suggested activities on the left-hand pages share common colors with their corresponding content on the right-hand pages. For example, references to ASL signs are always indicated in blue whether they appear in the "Signs" column, under their corresponding illustrations, or in the Sign Index. The following keys apply to all activities.

Lyrics

Look for this graphic above the words to the song.
In no time you'll be singing along!

Signs (and vocalizations)

This graphic headline denotes the ASL signs you'll learn in each activity. When appropriate, we list fun vocalizations or sounds you can make in italics (Grrr........)!

Notes about transparency and arrows

Positions illustrated as semi-transparent represent the starting position in a sign. Opaque positions indicate where the sign ends.

Single Movement

Double Movement
(Repeat)

Back and Forth Movement

Again

How to Use This Activity Guidebook

Activity Overview
The concept for each song is clearly explained in a short, easy-to-read paragraph. Whether it's learning food signs, animal signs, or opposites, the Activity Overview helps you get the most from each activity.

Lyrics, Signs & Vocalizations
Sign sequences are highlighted in blue to correspond with their sign demonstrations, making learning new signs easy. Some non-ASL "mime" or "movement" signs are marked in purple.

Sign Suggestions
Full-color illustrations of each suggested sign are presented in the order they first appear in the song, simplifying the learning and leading process.

Track 1

Brand New Day

Activity Overview

This activity encourages children to use their hands to mimic familiar daily activities: eating, dressing, hugging, combing hair, and brushing teeth. Note that the "Comb Hair" sign is relative to the hair of the signer. Long hair would dictate long strokes. But don't worry if your little ones don't have hair yet—or teeth—it's still great fun to pretend. As children begin to express themselves through signs, it truly is a "Brand New Day".

Notes from Joseph

Sign for "Morning"
The sign for "Morning," illustrated under Suggested Signs, is an artistic ASL sign that portrays the rising sun. It's perfectly appropriate to use this sign in the context of a song like "Brand New Day." However, in a typical ASL conversation, the alternate sign for "Morning," provided for reference purposes under Additional Signs, would normally be used.

Signs for "New" and "Day"
The signs for "New" and "Day" are provided under Additional Signs for anyone wanting to assist verbal language development by simultaneously reinforcing the spoken words "New" and "Day" with their ASL signs. However, in this song and in normal ASL conversation, the suggested sign for "Go forward into the day" reflects a more accurate ASL approach to communicating the idea of getting ready for a new day.

16

Lyrics

When we wake up in the mornin'
We can comb our hair, comb our hair
When we wake up in the mornin' we can comb our hair
And get ready for a brand new day

When we wake up in the mornin'
We can eat some food, eat some food
When we wake up in the mornin' we can eat some food
And get ready for a brand new day

When we wake up in the mornin'
We can brush our teeth, brush our teeth
When we wake up in the mornin' we can brush our teeth
And get ready for a brand new day

When we wake up in the mornin'
We can put on our clothes, put on our clothes
When we wake up in the mornin' we can put on our clothes
And get ready for a brand new day

Ready oooooo
Ready ahhhhh
Ready for a brand new day

When we wake up in the mornin'
I can give you a hug, give you a hug
When we wake up in the mornin' I can give you a hug
Then we're ready for a brand new day
Yes we're ready for a brand new day
Now we're ready for a brand new day

Activity Signs

Brand New Day

SIGN *with your* BABY®
author, Dr. Joseph Garcia, signs "Wake Up!"

Wake Up · Morning · Comb Hair · Ready

Go Forward (into the day) · Eat · Brush Teeth · Put on Clothes

Hug

Additional Signs

Morning · New · Day

17

Joseph's ASL Notes
Dr. Joseph Garcia, ASL educator and author of the book, SIGN *with your* BABY,® offers his expert tips and insight into the world of American Sign Language as it relates to each song.

Simple Signing
The baby icon indicates signs to use for a simpler interpretation of the songs. This alternate approach for leading children who are young or developmentally delayed, provides a more bite-sized means of achieving signing success quickly.

Additional Signs
Some of these signs can be added to the suggested signs to create more complex interpretations of the songs. This can help keep children challenged and engaged as they develop their signing skills. Others represent alternative ASL vocabulary.

How to Use This Activity Guidebook

Signing Options

The signs we suggest and illustrate represent one of many approaches to interpreting our songs. Consider the developmental stage of your children, your comfort level, and your proficiency when deciding which signs to introduce. For example, when signing to an audience comprised exclusively of very young children, 7 months to 12 months old, it may be more effective to introduce fewer signs per song than illustrated. We use a baby icon 🐮 on the sign illustrations to highlight choices we recommend for simple signing. You can just repeat these signs until the next highlighted sign is indicated by the music, in the same way as you might finger play "Spider," during the entire phrase, "the itsy bitsy spider crawled up the water spout." Some of the more complex songs have no baby icons because we found no effective way to simplify the approach any further than the suggested signs.

Helpful hint: For signing with older or more dexterous children, you may want to add more signs for each song. We've provided some "Additional Signs" for those wanting a more advanced or alternate song interpretation. Remember that these exercises are designed for fun and to develop both ASL and spoken vocabularies. For this objective, there are many "appropriate" ways to interpret the songs.

The song sequence is largely organized in order of age appropriateness, starting with songs for your youngest signers. However, you may find your first-graders signing "Please Change My Diaper" and getting a healthy laugh. Don't assume that the lyrics of a song will exclude it from being of interest to older children. Let your children be the judge and use their enthusiasm to help you decide which songs to teach next.

Encourage Creativity

Some songs offer the option of having the children mime, or act out, the actions indicated in the song. For example, in "Let's Go Riding," children can pretend to be airplanes during the "riding in a big airplane" phrase. Some songs, such as "Jumping Up and Down," combine movement with signs. Here, children jump up and down, then sign "Frog." Invite your children to explore their own style and movements by asking, "How would you hop like a frog?" Encourage them to use their creativity!

Maintain a Positive Attitude

Whenever you lead an activity with a group of children, it's important to create an environment that welcomes and encourages active participation, but does not force it. This program has been designed with fun in mind and should not be presented as a drill. Our suggested activities will be more enjoyable for everyone if approached with a joyful, playful, and flexible attitude. Create an environment where your children will want to participate.

Prepare In Advance

As with most endeavors, better preparation results in a better experience. Before you lead any of the Sign2Me activities, we suggest that you take the following steps that are also covered in the "How to Learn an Activity" and "How to Lead an Activity" training videos on your Enhanced CD:

Learn the Activity

- Read the Activity Overview and identify its corresponding CD track number.

- Read the lyrics and sign sequences as you listen to the song.

- Read "Joseph's ASL Notes" to determine if any of the "Additional Signs" are appropriate for you and your children.

- Review and learn the signs you will introduce with the song, taking into account the age of your children, their skill development and your proficiency.

- Review and practice each one of the signs you have chosen.

- If possible, practice in front of a mirror. That way, you can see just how your signs will appear to your audience so you can fine-tune your approach.

- Listen to the song again, this time signing along with the music. Use the music to guide your pacing of the signs.

Once you are comfortable with signing the song, you are ready to introduce it to a group. We suggest the following approach:

Lead the Activity

- Begin by teaching the sign for "Applause" (see illustration at Right). You can use this sign after every song to celebrate your efforts.

- If this is your first time leading a group, select one of the songs with the fewest signs. We suggest "Brand New Day" or "Pick Me Up!"

- Walk through the entire sequence of signs with your children before the music is played. Repeat each sign a few times to help the children get comfortable with the movements. Provide extra guidance to those who need it.

- Play the song and demonstrate the signs as you go. Don't worry if the children don't use the signs at the appropriate times (or if they don't sign at all). Laugh and have fun – even if you make mistakes yourself!

- Most importantly, acknowledge your children's successes. Celebrate their efforts with rounds of signed applause and praise.

Acknowledge your children's successes. Celebrate their efforts with rounds of signed applause and praise.

Listen to Your Children

- Honor your children's requests to listen to the same song over and over. After all, repetition is an important key to this style of learning! Fortunately, we produced the music to be enjoyed by adults, too.

- Incorporate the signs you've learned into other daily activities.

- Choose new songs from the CD to learn and teach according to the ages and interests of your little signers.

  Helpful hint: Play the CD for listening enjoyment too, or as background music for other activities so children can become familiar with the lyrics and the music. This will help them, and you, select which songs to learn next.

Make Room!

If you will be working with a group of children, or a group of children and adults, make sure there is enough elbow room so the activities don't become an exercise in conflict resolution. More space is needed for large-movement activities like, "There's a Tiger Walking" and "Let's Go Riding." Many leaders find it fun to simply walk, mime and sign around the room in a big line during these activities.

Right vs. Left-Hand Dominance

American Sign Language does not require the use of a specific hand, right or left, for the actions of the signs. It's important to be consistent however so that during a song, you don't use your left hand for the action hand part of the time, and your right hand for the rest. We suggest that you don't mention the matter

Author of **SIGN** *with your* **BABY**, Joseph Garcia speaking with a group of parents and teachers

to your little signers unless it comes up. They will instinctively use their naturally dominant hand. We chose to illustrate all signs with a right action hand, but this was for consistency only.

Sing While You Sign

Once you are familiar with the lyrics, singing while you sign is recommended. If you don't like singing, we encourage you to at least imitate the animals and other sounds included in some of the songs. These songs are designed to encourage vocalization from the children who will be inclined to follow your example. The more you howl and roar, the more fun it will be for you and your children. Besides, if you sing you may discover your hidden talent!

Sign In Your Daily Activities

Using signs in a variety of appropriate contexts is an important aspect of helping children discover the meaning of those signs. For example, when a child hears and sees you say and sign "More" at every mealtime, and also at playtime and reading time, then she will begin to associate the term "More" with getting more of whatever is currently happening, not just food. Very young children can learn to sign to music, but seeing these signs used by adults in a variety of other contexts during their daily activities will help them learn to use the signs to express their own observations and desires when it makes the most sense for them. Remember: Although learning these signs with music can be viewed as performing to some extent, we would never recommend that you have preverbal children perform signs as an amusement for other adults. Requests from adults like, "Hey Brian, do that elephant sign for Uncle John..." may serve to confuse rather than reinforce the sign's meaning, unless there just happens to be an elephant right there in the living room!

English and American Sign Language

American Sign Language (ASL) is the primary language for people who are deaf in the United States and Canada. It is not a visual form of the English language and its structure (syntax and grammar) is significantly different from English. In addition to hand movements, it incorporates body movement, direction, eye contact, facial expression, body posturing, pantomime, space, and context to convey meaning. While in English we might say, "Do you want to go to the beach?" a person using ASL might sign, "Beach, You/Me, Together-Go-There" with an inquisitive expression that defines the phrase as a question.

Simultaneous and direct translation between English and ASL is a challenge and in some cases, virtually impossible. The challenge is greatest when attempting to use signs to strengthen the connection between a sign and its corresponding spoken word to help build pre-verbal, hearing children's vocabularies. Another form of sign language known as manual English is best for English vocabulary building. When translating between any two languages, often one word in a language can require several words in the second language to convey similar meaning. Some signs in ASL require several English words to achieve shared meaning. Likewise, it may require several signs to give equal meaning for a spoken word. Languages also borrow words from one another to satisfy communication needs. Going from a spoken to manual language creates its own set of challenges.

Striking a Balance

Since there is not always a one-to-one English-word to ASL-sign correlation, and since full ASL translations for each song would not provide the simultaneous spoken reinforcement for the signs, we struck a good balance. Our solution was to create sign sequences for the songs that convey the main ideas of each lyrical phrase. We also included the Additional Signs for those wanting alternative interpretations. Joseph's ASL Notes are designed to raise awareness about specific ASL issues relevant to each song.

Manual English is a category of visual gestural languages that use ASL signs, in combination with new or modified signs, to enable signing in English word order and sentence structure. Manual English is widely used in educational programs for children with special needs. Along with ASL, Manual English is often introduced to children who are deaf to assist them in learning English.

If a sign language interpreter for either ASL or a Manual English language were to interpret our songs for an adult audience of people who are deaf, neither would use the simplified method we've outlined in this activity guidebook. This resource is designed to introduce simple ASL vocabulary to hearing children while listening to fun music. The objective is for children to increase their ASL and spoken English vocabularies while enjoying and being prompted by playful music and physical activities.

Helpful hint: As you start signing with children, you may discover that you really enjoy using ASL. ASL is truly a gift from the Deaf community! You can learn more about this rich and beautiful language by taking an ASL course at your local community college or resource centers that support the Deaf community.

Give Us Your Feedback

We value your thoughts about the music and activities in "Li'L Pick Me Up!" Your feedback will help make future volumes even better. Please e-mail us at customerservice@sign2me.com to share your experiences and comments or to offer suggestions. We welcome pictures and stories of you and your children enjoying the Li'L Pick Me Up! Enhanced Music CD and Activity book.

Information about additional Sign2Me products is provided on the last page of this book and on your Enhanced CD. New product releases and additional learning and teaching resources are also found on our web site at www.sign2me.com.

Track 1

Brand New Day

Activity Overview

This activity encourages children to use their hands to mimic familiar daily activities: eating, dressing, hugging, combing hair, and brushing teeth. Note that the "Comb Hair" sign is relative to the hair of the signer. Long hair would dictate long strokes. But don't worry if your little ones don't have hair yet—or teeth—it's still great fun to pretend. As children begin to express themselves through signs, it truly is a "Brand New Day".

Notes from Joseph

Sign for "Morning"
The sign for "Morning," illustrated under Suggested Signs, is an artistic ASL sign that portrays the rising sun. It's perfectly appropriate to use this sign in the context of a song like "Brand New Day." However, in a typical ASL conversation, the alternate sign for "Morning," provided for reference purposes under Additional Signs, would normally be used.

Signs for "New" and "Day"
The signs for "New" and "Day" are provided under Additional Signs for anyone wanting to assist verbal language development by simultaneously reinforcing the spoken words "New" and "Day" with their ASL signs. However, in this song and in normal ASL conversation, the suggested sign for "Go forward into the day" reflects a more accurate ASL approach to communicating the idea of getting ready for a new day.

Lyrics

When we wake up in the mornin'
We can comb our hair, comb our hair
When we wake up in the mornin' we can comb our hair
And get ready for a brand new day

When we wake up in the mornin'
We can eat some food, eat some food
When we wake up in the mornin' we can eat some food
And get ready for a brand new day

When we wake up in the mornin'
We can brush our teeth, brush our teeth
When we wake up in the mornin' we can brush our teeth
And get ready for a brand new day

When we wake up in the mornin'
We can put on our clothes, put on our clothes
When we wake up in the mornin' we can put on our clothes
And get ready for a brand new day

Ready oooooo
Ready ahhhhh
Ready for a brand new day

When we wake up in the mornin'
I can give you a hug, give you a hug
When we wake up in the mornin' I can give you a hug
Then we're ready for a brand new day
Yes we're ready for a brand new day
Now we're ready for a brand new day

Activity Signs
Brand New Day

Wake Up — *eyes pop open*

Morning — *like the sun rising*

Comb Hair

Ready — *use the "R" hand shape*

Go Forward *(into the day)*

Eat

Brush Teeth

Put on Clothes

Hug

Additional Signs

Morning

New

Day

17

Pick Me Up!

Lyrics

I want up, up, up
Pick me up, up, up
I want up, up, up
Please Momma
Pick me up

I want more, more, more
Give me more, more, more
I want more, more, more
Please Daddy, I want more

I want more food
I want more play
I want more you, you, you
Today

I want up, up, up
Pick me up, up, up
I want up, up, up
Please Momma
Pick me up

Come on, come on...
Hey baby, get up outta that high chair and give me a solo!

I want more food
I want more play
I want more you, you, you
Today

I want up, up, up
Pick me up, up, up
I want up, up, up
Please Momma
Pick me up

Yeah yeah yeah, Pick me up
Please pick me up
Come on pick me up
Don't let me down, no no no no
Don't let me down
Please pick me up

Activity Overview

This is a great song to introduce to new signers. It may require several exposures before the youngest children become accustomed to its fast pace. Through repetition, it reinforces signs for familiar and important concepts, including "Up," "Mommy," "More," "Daddy," "Food" and "Play." Though designed for the youngest signers, its catchy melody and soulful lead vocal are enough to pick everyone up!

Notes from Joseph

The activity leader can easily add the Additional Signs into the appropriate places in the song. For children under 15 months, I suggest you let them try the Suggested Signs first, then add more signs as their signing skills improve. I like starting with the "Up" sign and ending the phrase with the "Pick Me Up!" sign when "Pick Me Up!" is sung.

Pick Me Up!

● Mime or movement

Toddler, Emma, signs "Up"

Up

Mommy

More

tap fingers together

Daddy

Food

Play

You

Today

hands move down then bounce at end

Not Down

Additional Signs

Please

Pick Me Up

Want

19

Track 3
Please Change My Diaper

Activity Overview

Wouldn't it be great if infants could tell you when they need their diapers changed? Well, it won't be long now, because this song introduces the signs to do just that! There's no need to sign the tongue-in-cheek song commentary—though some classes have resorted to plugging their nose and making a stinky grimace at the song's end. Remember to have fun with this! Now the only question is, cloth or disposable?

Notes from Joseph

In this song, the idea of "Need" can be expressed by making an urgent facial expression while signing "Change." As signing skills develop, the sign "Need" can be added. It is included in Additional Signs. Until then, hamming it up with your face and your expressions will help each sign convey even more meaning. We use the sign for "Dirty" rather than the sign for "Full" because it is more descriptive. We added "Full" to the Additional Signs for those wanting a literal translation.

Lyrics

Hey kids, thanks for coming out. It's nice to see you spend your nap time with me. Hey Charlie! Good to see you. Trixie! Bring over some of your best formula for my friends at table 23.

Here's a little something we all know about.

When my diaper's wet I can tell you
When my diaper's wet I can say
When my diaper's wet I can tell you
That my diaper needs to be changed
Please change my diaper, it needs to be changed
Please change my diaper, my diaper needs to be changed

You know, to have change, you really must want it.

When my diaper's full I can tell you
When my diaper's full I can say
When my diaper's full I can tell you
That my diaper needs to be changed
Please change my diaper, it needs to be changed
Please change my diaper, my diaper needs to be changed

Please change my diaper, it needs to be changed
Please change my diaper, my diaper needs to be changed
It needs to be changed

Why else would it smell like that in here?
Hey, you're the one who fed me all the dietary fiber.

I've had Limburger that smells better than this.
Somebody crack a window, I'm dyin' in here.

Light a match or somethin'…

Please Change My Diaper

Joseph models the
sign for "Change"

Diaper

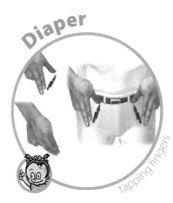

tapping fingers

Wet

tapping fingers

Tell / Say

Change

hands switch places

Dirty

wiggle fingers

Additional
Signs

My

Need

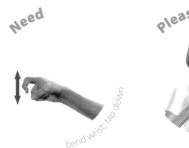

bend wrist; tap down

Please

Full

palm brushes top of fist

Track 4
More Milk

Activity Overview

Hungry? This song features several popular foods for young children. When made near the breast, the "Milk" sign is also appropriate for breast-feeding. This song was written with the idea that repetition is the key to learning. Repetition is the key to learning. Repeti…you get the idea. The Bonus Song, "More..." on our Enhanced CD is the same song but without lyrics for the food and drink items so you can sing it karaoke-style with your own choice of nouns. See page 9 to learn how to access it. Page 56-57 has the activity plan and a selection of illustrations.

Notes from Joseph

In order to make the sign "More" work within the quick pace of this song, just tap your fingertips together once. You can indicate that you are asking a question by raising your eyebrows with an inquisitive expression. "More Milk?" I recommend the sign "Drink" rather than "Juice," because "Drink" is a sign commonly used for "Juice" and the littlest hands have a tough time using their pinkies effectively to make the "Juice" sign. Also, "Juice" is typically signed as a specific type of juice, such as apple or orange. This would require you to perform two signs in the space of one syllable in this song. For reference, an illustration for "Juice" is provided under Additional Signs.

Lyrics

More milk
More milk
Please may I have more milk?
More milk
More milk
Please may I have more milk?
For mine's all gone
I want more milk

More juice
More juice
Please may I have more juice?
More juice
More juice
Please may I have more juice?
For mine's all gone
I want more juice

More crackers
More crackers
Please may I have more crackers?
More crackers
More crackers
Please may I have more crackers?
For mine's all gone
I want more crackers

More water
More water
Please may I have more water?
More water
More water
Please may I have more water?
For mine's all gone
I want more water

More apples
More apples
Please may I have more apples?
More apples
More apples
Please may I have more apples?
For mine's all gone
I want more apples

More cheese
More cheese
Please may I have more cheese
More cheese
More cheese
Please may I have more cheese
For mine's all gone
For mine's all gone
For mine's all gone
I want more cheese

Activity Signs
More Milk

Ana models the sign for "Milk"

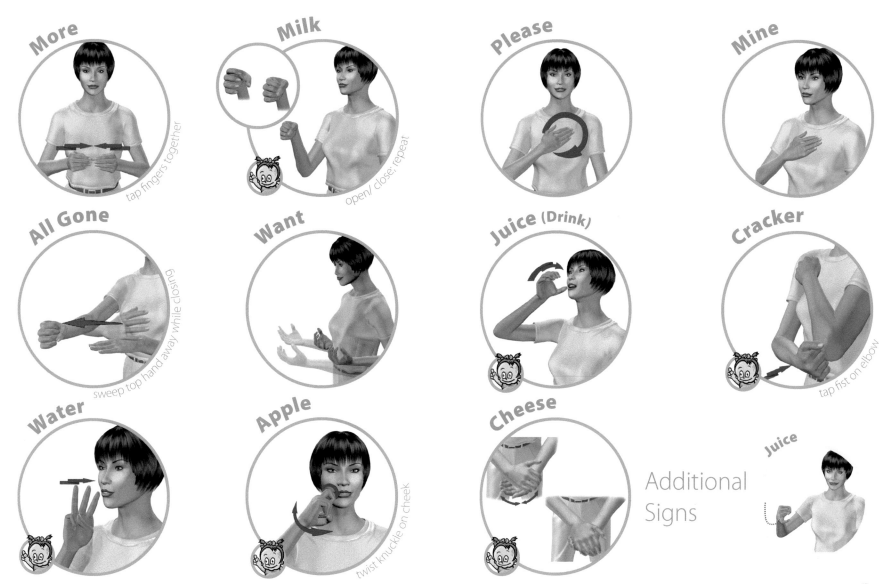

More
tap fingers together

Milk
open/ close; repeat

Please

Mine

All Gone
sweep top hand away while closing

Want

Juice (Drink)

Cracker
tap fist on elbow

Water

Apple
twist knuckle on cheek

Cheese

Additional Signs

Juice

Track 5
There's a Tiger Walking

Activity Overview

You've got options with this song. We suggest you start with the activity as illustrated here. Children make the signs for each animal then mimic the animal's sounds. For another approach, have children move in a circle around the room, mimicking the movement and sound of each animal: a tiger walking through the jungle, a snake sliding through the forest, a monkey swinging, etc. Let us know when you've got a good sound for a hippo.

Notes from Joseph

Sometimes an object is shown through mime, instead of using the formal sign, to define its relationship to the subject of the sentence. For example, in Additional Signs, we include two signs for "Flower." The first represents the flower using one hand, through mime, to show the bee is buzzing in it. The second illustrates the formal ASL sign for flower.

Lyrics

There's a tiger walkin' through the jungle
There's a tiger walkin' all around
There's a tiger walkin' through the jungle
And he makes the scariest sound

There's a snake slidin' through the forest
There's a snake slidin' all around
There's a snake slidin' through the forest
And he makes the hissiest sound

There's a monkey swingin' through the treetops
There's a monkey swingin' all around
There's a monkey swingin' through the treetops
And he makes the swinginest sound

There's a hippo swimmin' in the river
There's a hippo swimmin' all around
There's a hippo swimmin' in the river
He makes a hippopotamus sound

There's a bee buzzin' in the flowers,
There's a bee buzzin' all around
There's a bee buzzin' in the flowers,
And it makes the buzzinest sound

Activity Signs
There's a Tiger Walking

● Mime or movement

Tiger

Walk (Like a Tiger)

Voice

Hear

Snake (Sliding)

Monkey

Swing in Tree

like a monkey

Hippo

Swim

Bee

fingers brush past cheek

Buzzing (Flying)

Additional Signs

Jungle (Forest, Trees)

River

Buzzing in Flower

like a bee in a flower

Flower

25

Track 6
Get Up and Shake

Activity Overview

Here's a way to get those sillies out—especially on a rainy day! Kids can shake their hands, jump up and down, reach up high to the sky, and fall down. To prevent injuries, we suggest crouching instead of really falling! During the last few verses, you can "Reach Up High" from a crouching position. Make sure children who are mobile have enough room to move without bumping into each other and causing a ruckus. "Get Up and Fight" is not nearly as much fun.

Notes from Joseph

Careful: If you want to move pre-mobile babies' bodies in rhythm to this song, please be careful! Never lift or swing babies by their hands. It's too easy to cause harm to their small, undeveloped muscles and joints.

Lyrics

Get up and shake, shake, shake, shake your hands
Jump, jump, jump, up and down
Reach up high, to the sky, and now fall down

Get up and shake, shake, shake, shake your hands
Jump, jump, jump, up and down
Reach up high, to the sky, and now fall down

Get up and shake, shake, shake, shake your hands
Jump, jump, jump, up and down
Reach up high, to the sky, and now fall down

Everybody roll around now

Get up and shake, shake, shake, shake your hands
Jump, jump, jump, up and down
Reach up high, to the sky, and now fall down

Get up and shake, shake, shake, shake your hands
Jump, jump, jump, come on and jump up and down
Reach up high, to the sky, and now fall down
Reach up high, to the sky, and now fall down
Reach up high, to the sky, and now fall down

Get Up and Shake

● Mime or movement

The class celebrates by signing "Applause"

Shake Your Hands

Jump Up and Down

Reach Up High

Crouch Down (fall down)

Roll Around (On the Floor)

Track 7
Where is Baby's Tummy?

Activity Overview

"Where?" is a very useful sign for young children. Ask them to indicate where each body part is and you've got a fun game. When you first introduce this song and its signs, start by using the signs as we've listed them here, pointing to the body parts on yourself and then your child, on the line "It's right there." If you're teaching a class of children, just point to your own body parts. Once they become more familiar with spoken words, use the "Where" sign only while singing "Where is baby's tummy (nose, mouth, toes)?" letting them point to their body parts without any gestural hint from you. For older children who don't wish to be identified as babies, try using a doll as the baby.

Notes from Joseph

In ASL, body parts are usually identified by pointing or drawing a quick circle around them. One exception is "Toes," which has its own ASL sign. Because using your hands to talk about toes might be confusing to preverbal infants, I just point across the toes. For anyone interested, another sign for "Toes" is under Additional Signs. Now everybody knows.

Lyrics

Where is baby's tummy?
Can you show me where?
Where is baby's tummy?
It's right there (point to tummy)

Where is baby's nose?
Can you show me where?
Where is baby's nose?
It's right there (point to nose)

Where is baby's mouth?
Can you show me where?
Where is baby's mouth?
It's right there (point to mouth)

Where are baby's toes?
Can you show me where?
Where are baby's toes?
They're right there (point to toes)

Time for a little review now

Here is baby's tummy
Here is baby's nose
Here is baby's mouth
Now everybody knows

Where is baby's tummy?
Can you show me where?
Where is baby's tummy?
It's right there! (point to tummy)

Activity Signs
Where is Baby's Tummy?

Sienna shows us her "Tummy".

Where

finger moves from side to side

Tummy

Show Me

move toward body

Nose

Mouth

Toes

Again

(Again sign illustration)

Everybody

(Everybody sign illustration)

Know

Additional Signs

Toes

Baby

Hear the Little Doggie

Activity Overview

Here's a chance to combine familiar animal signs with animal sounds. Try making the specific "Animal Sound" sign at the same time that you voice that animal sound. The more animated you are, the more fun it will be for your little ones.

Notes from Joseph

There are two different signs for "Hear" and "Listen," but for the youngest signers, it's better to start with just one. Using the signs for both "Hear" and "Listen" with older children will help them understand the subtle differences between the meanings of these closely-related words.

Lyrics

Hear the little doggie, listen to it say
Woof, woof, woof, woof, woof all day

Hear the little cow, listen to it say
Moo, moo, moo, moo, moo all day

Hear the little pig, listen to it say
Oink, oink, oink, oink, oink all day

Hear the little kitty, listen to it say
Meow, meow, meow, meow, meow all day

Hear the little birdie, listen to it say
Tweet, tweet, tweet, tweet, tweet all day

Hear the little doggie, listen to it say
Woof, woof, woof, woof, woof all day

Woof, woof, woof, woof, woof all day
Woof, woof, woof, woof, woof all day

Hear the Little Doggie

● Mime or movement

Toddler, Cadence, approximates the sign for "Bird"

Hear

Dog

pat leg

Voice

Animal Sound

open and close hand while making sound

All Day

Cow

Pig

Cat

Bird

tap open and closed several times

Additional Signs

Listen

Say

31

I Said Oww!

Lyrics

I was sitting by the door, I just got out of bed
When suddenly the door swung open
And bonked me in the head
And I said, "Ooooowwww, my head hurts, my head hurts
My head hurts"
I said, "Ooooowwww, my head hurts," and I signed, "Stop,"
Please don't hit my head again

I was listening to music, its what I like to hear
When suddenly my friend, yelled right into my ear
And I said, "Ooooowwww, my ear hurts, my ear hurts, my ear hurts"
I said, "Ooooowwww, my ear hurts," and I signed, "Stop,"
Please don't yell in my ear again

Now that's some nice pickin'. Can't hear it if my ear hurts.

One day I ate some cookies, I ate them for my lunch
But because I ate so many
My tummy ached a bunch
And I said, "Ooooowwww, my tummy hurts, my tummy hurts
My tummy hurts"
I said, "Ooooowwww, my tummy hurts"
Now I don't eat so many cookies for my lunch

One day when I was walking, as happy as can be
Suddenly a tricycle rolled right into my knee
And I said, "Ooooowwww, my knee hurts, my knee hurts
My knee hurts"
I said, "Ooooowwww, my knee hurts"
Please bring a little hug and kiss to me
Please bring another hug and kiss to me
So won't you bring a little hug and kiss to me…Oww!

Activity Overview

This country-style tune introduces children to the notion of placing the sign for "Pain" near a part of their body that's been hurt. It also encourages them to sign "Stop," after being bonked, as an alternative to biting or hitting. The more you ham it up when howling "Ooooowww!", the more fun it is for the kids and it also helps preverbal children exercise their young vocal cords. Try to time the mime actions with their corresponding sound effect. This pantomime activity is a hoot for everyone—even seasoned cowpokes.

Notes from Joseph

In ASL, mime is frequently the most effective way to show an action that happens in a story. Concepts such as "Suddenly" can easily be conveyed through body language by sudden movements. This also makes ASL a fun language to use and to watch. Before you begin this activity, ask your children to demonstrate what it's like to be bonked in the head, or hit by a tricycle. Give them the chance to be the center of attention and to use their imaginations to describe a painful experience through movement.

Activity Signs
I Said Oww!

● Mime or movement

Door Swings Open (and Hits Head)

Hurt (General)

tap fingers together

Hurt (Specific)

Stop

Sit

like legs on a chair

Rub Eyes

Not Again

shake head "no"

Hear

Music

Friend

hook fingers

Yell into Ear

Eat

Cookie

Lunch

Eating a Lot
●

Tummy Ache
●

Walk

Happy
brush up on chest

Bike (Tricycle)

Roll into Knee
●

Hug

Kiss

33

Look Up, Look Down

Lyrics

Look up, I see a butterfly
Look up, I see a bird in the sky
Look up, I see the clouds go floating by

Look down, I see a worm on the ground
Look down, come see the bug I found
I'm so happy when you're around

Butterfly, a bird in the sky, the clouds go floating by
Worm on the ground, a bug I found
I'm happy when you're around

Look up, I see a butterfly
Look down, I see a worm on the ground
I'm so happy when you're around
I'm so happy when you're around
I'm so happy when you're around

Activity Overview

Pointing is one of the first and best ways children communicate what they are observing. Here we take this concept one step further by focusing attention on sight ("Look") and on direction ("Up" and "Down"). The sign for "Look" is directional, modified by either pointing the sign upward when you sing the words "Look Up," or downward when you sing "Look Down." This song is a special favorite because of the beautiful signs for those items that catch the attention of little explorers.

Notes from Joseph

People frequently ask why words like "So" don't get signed. That's because "So" in this song can better be conveyed with facial expressions while you make the sign for "Happy." Try it. Practice making the "Happy" sign in a normal happy way. Then try making the same sign and put some pizzazz in it to convey "So Happy."

Look Up, Look Down

Pre-K, Matthew, signs
"Butterfly"

Look Up

Butterfly — *flutter fingers*

Bird — *tap open and closed several times*

Clouds

Look Down

Worm

Bug

Happy — *brush up on chest*

You

Around

Additional Signs

Sky

I

Track 11
When It's Cold Outside

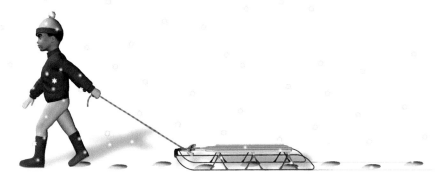

Activity Overview

Children imitate the motions of getting dressed to go outside in the cold. Use the ASL sign for "Cold" (it's perfectly descriptive), but for the rest of the suggested movements, just imitate the movement of putting on various garments. The challenge—and fun—is to keep up. Can you?

Notes from Joseph

Young children will most likely prefer to ignore the sign for "Outside." But for those who want that extra vocabulary word, you've got it. Remember to pull the action-hand "Out" in the direction of "Outdoors" as you make this sign.

Lyrics

"Ooooooh. It's a little nippy out there, so what're we going to do?"

When it's cold outside I put on my coat,
I put on my coat when it's cold
When it's cold outside I put on my hat,
I put on my hat when it's cold
I put on my coat, I put on my hat when it's cold outside

When it's cold outside I put on my mittens,
I put on my mittens when it's cold
When it's cold outside I put on my boots,
I put on my boots when it's cold
I put on my mittens, I put on my boots when it's cold outside

Let's play it now… Oooh Baby, when it's cold outside.
Its so nippy, I need a little tawny I think?
Now you young ones, you bundle up, you hear?
I'll give you a peanut butter and 'nanner sandwich in a minute.

When it's cold outside I put on my coat,
I put on my coat when it's cold
When it's cold outside I put on my hat,
I put on my hat when it's cold
I put on my coat, I put on my hat when it's cold outside

When it's cold outside I put on my mittens,
I put on my mittens when it's cold
When it's cold outside I put on my boots,
I put on my boots when it's cold
I put on my mittens, I put on my boots when it's cold outside

What Else?

I put on my coat, I put on my hat when it's cold outside
I put on my mittens, I put on my boots when it's cold outside

Oohh baby, it's cold out there! Thank you, thank you very much.
Oh, can't be leavin' the building yet, I gotta find my coat and my hat, and
my mittens and my boots, and my latte' and my scarf, where's my scarf
and my earmuffs and my moonboots….

When It's Cold Outside

● Mime or movement

Claire and her Mom sign "Cold" while reading a story

Cold

Put on Coat

Put on Hat

Put on Mittens

Put on Boots

Additional Signs

Outside

move hand in direction of outside

Track 12
Go to the Zoo

Activity Overview

Signs for animals are always a hit with young ones. This beautiful song combines some of the most beloved and easily identifiable animals in a melody that you'll be humming in the shower and at the zoo. This song also provides a unique opportunity to learn how ASL uses space in front of the body to convey meaning. See Joseph's ASL Notes for more.

Tip: Listen through headphones for guaranteed goose bumps!

Notes from Joseph

One advantage of American Sign Language is that it uses space to help convey meaning. You can place things in a space in front of you by pointing, fingerspelling or using signs called "classifiers." Then, you can refer to them by pointing to that space or moving signs toward that space. In this song, when your fingers spell "Z-O-O" for zoo, spell it well out in front of you in a specific location. Then, during the phrase, "I'll go there with you," take the "With You" sign and move it to the place where you spelled zoo. Get the idea? During musical interludes that have no words, try introducing the "Music" sign.

Lyrics

Do you want to go to the zoo? I'll go there with you
We can see the crocodiles, and the tigers too

Do you want to go to the zoo? I'll go there with you
We can see the tall giraffes, and the lions too

Animals, animals, lots of animals at the zoo
Animals, animals, I will go to the zoo with you

Do you want to go to the zoo? I'll go there with you
We can see the timber wolves, and the brown bears too

Do you want to go to the zoo? I'll go there with you
We can see the elephants and the monkeys too

Animals, animals, lots of animals at the zoo
Animals, animals, I will go to the zoo with you

Do you want to go to the zoo? I'll go there with you
We can see the crocodiles, and the tigers too
We can see the tall giraffes, and the lions too
We can see the timber wolves, and the brown bears too
We can see the elephants and the monkeys too

Go to the Zoo

Go

Z-O-O
finger spell Z-O-O

Go There Together
hands move forward together

See

Crocodile
crock mouth open and close

Tiger
like stripes on a tiger's face

Giraffe
depicts long neck

Lion
lion's mane

Animal

Wolf

Bear
like claws scratching

Elephant

Monkey

Additional Signs

Want

Many (Lots of Animals)

Music

Sometimes When I am Hungry

Activity Overview

This activity helps children, teachers and parents learn the signs for common foods. It's not a menu for the ideal diet for a young child, but we've included many favorites. Through repetition, children will also begin to recognize the difference between hunger and thirst. As a related exercise, use these signs at other times during your day whenever hunger, thirst, or bananas appear.

Notes from Joseph

I recommend you use the suggested signs for young children. Once they are familiar with the basic version, add "When" and "Now." Don't forget to raise those eyebrows when you ask for something.

Lyrics

Sometimes when I am hungry, I like to eat a cracker
Right now I'm very hungry, may I have a cracker please

Sometimes when I am thirsty, I like to drink some water
Right now I'm very thirsty, may I have some water please

Sometimes when I am hungry, I like to eat some apple
Right now I'm very hungry, may I have some apple please

Sometimes when I am thirsty, I like to drink some milk
Right now I'm very thirsty, may I have some milk please

Sometimes when I am hungry, I like to eat some banana
Right now I'm very hungry, may I have a banana please

I say thank you

I say thank you

I say thank you

Thank you

Sometimes When I am Hungry

Monta and Sirena sign "Eat" before their picnic

Hungry

Eat

Cracker
tap fist on elbow

Please

Thirsty

Drink

Water

Apple
twist knuckles on cheek

Milk
Open - close, repeat

Banana
peeling motion

Thank You

Additional Signs

When

Now

Like

41

See the Birdie Flying

Lyrics

See the birdie flying high
See the birdie flying low
See it flying high, see it flying low
See the birdie flying

Fly high, fly low
See the birdie flying
(Repeat)

See the kitty walking quickly
See the kitty walking slowly
See it walking fast, see it walking slow
See the kitty walking

Walk fast, walk slow
See the kitty walking
(Repeat)

See the bunny hopping in
See the bunny hopping out
See it hopping in, see it hopping out
See the bunny hopping

Hop in, Hop out
See the bunny hopping
(Repeat)

Hear the children clapping softly
Hear the children clapping loudly
Hear them clapping soft
Hear them clapping loud
Hear the children clapping

Clap soft, clap loud
Hear the children clapping
(Repeat)

Fly high, Fly low
Walk fast, walk slow
Hop in, hop out
Clap soft, clap loud
Now this song is finished

Activity Overview

Animals and opposites are the focus here: birdie flying high and low, kitty walking fast and slow, bunny hopping in and out. As an alternative to signing during a circle-time activity, children can pretend to fly with arms outstretched, then walk fast and slow. Remember to request they go along the line of the circle no faster than the person in front of them. They can hop in and hop out of the circle, and clap along. We found three claps work best.

Notes from Joseph

A sign can be made at different speeds or in different locations depending on its context. The hands are above the head for "Fly High" and lower for "Fly Low." The sign for "Walk Fast" is just like "Walk Slow," only faster—get the idea? When introducing this song to children, you can refer to it as the opposite song, and show them the sign for opposite, illustrated under Additional Signs.

See the Birdie Flying

● Mime or movement

Kindergartner, Dylan, signs
"Bird" on the playground

Bird — tap open and closed several times

Fly High — fingers flap high

Fly Low — fingers flap low

Cat — like stroking a cat's whiskers

Walk

Bunny

Hop In

Hop Out

Children — like tapping on heads

Clap Soft ●

Clap Loud ●

Music

Finished

Additional Signs

See

Opposite — fingers move away from center

43

Let's Take a Little Walk

Activity Overview

Going for a walk can be a rich learning experience for young children. This song is about taking a walk and discovering exciting activities that are happening around a tree. A bird sings in it, a butterfly flies around it, a squirrel climbs it, and children pick an apple from it to share. How many of these signs can you use the next time you're outside? Take a little walk and see!

Notes from Joseph

Asking a very young child to sign every meaning in a fast-paced song isn't practical or necessary. Take the phrase "furry little squirrel" for example. I don't know a squirrel that isn't furry, so it is assumed that the squirrel has fur. The Additional Signs are for those who want a few more descriptive signs. Lots of wonderful opportunities exist to use descriptive signs when walking outside.

Lyrics

What a day outside, what do you say…

Let's take a little walk outside
And see what we can see
Maybe we'll see a pretty little bird
Singing up in a tree

Do you think so, well let's take a little walk and see

Let's take a little walk outside
And see what we can see
Maybe we'll see a big butterfly
Flying around a tree

Let's take a little walk outside
And see what we can see
Maybe we'll see a furry little squirrel
Climbing around a tree

I can see him up there. He's got something in his hand.
I think it's a nut.

Let's take a little walk outside
And see what we can see
Maybe we'll pick an apple or two
Just for you and me

I dig apples. Do you like 'em? I like 'em.
I like apples and nuts.
I think we should go check out that squirrel.

Let's Take a Little Walk

● Mime or movement

Nickie and her class
take a little "Walk"

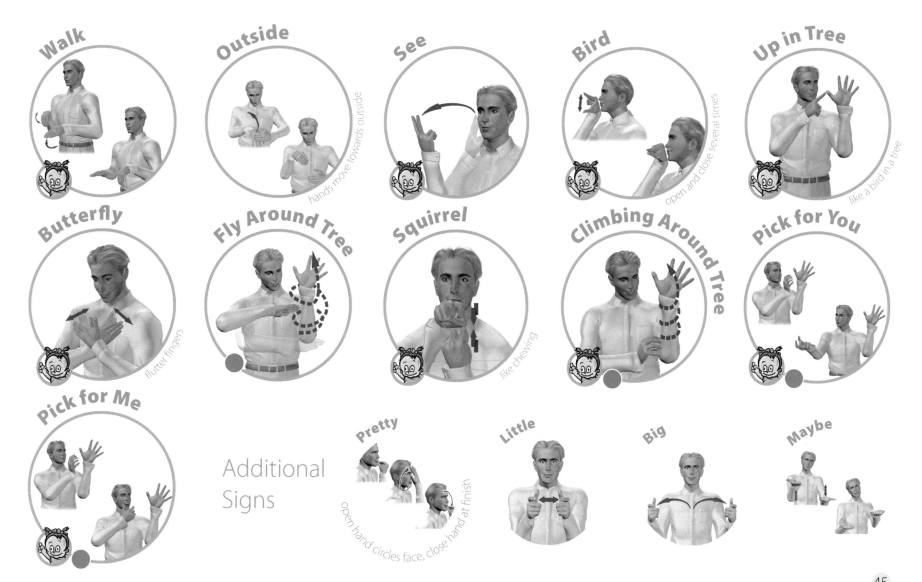

Walk

Outside
hands move towards outside

See

Bird
open and close several times

Up in Tree
like a bird in a tree

Butterfly
flutter fingers

Fly Around Tree

Squirrel
like chewing

Climbing Around Tree

Pick for You

Pick for Me

Additional
Signs

Pretty
open hand circles face, close hand at finish

Little

Big

Maybe

45

Talking on the Telephone

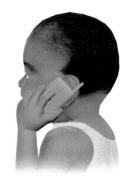

Activity Overview

Here's a chance to introduce the signs for referring to specific family members through a song with a cool calypso beat and lots of repetition. The pace of this song requires signers to stay alert and think ahead. Kids pretend to talk on the phone with their mommy, daddy, sister, brother, grandma, grandpa, and a friend. Soon they'll want their own extension!

Notes from Joseph

When interpreting phrases like "I'm talking on the telephone," it's not necessary to sign "I," "Talk" and "On." The one sign, "Telephone," represents the entire idea. Three options for "I Love You" are offered. For toddlers, the single-sign "Love" is sufficient. Second in difficulty is the three-sign version under Additional Signs. The single-sign version is frequently used to express this sentiment but requires significant dexterity. Who would have thought "Love" could be so complicated?

Lyrics

I'm talking on the telephone to my mommy, to my mommy, to my mommy
It's fun to talk on the telephone saying, "Mommy, I love you"

I'm talking on the telephone to my daddy, to my daddy, to my daddy
It's fun to talk on the telephone saying, "Daddy, I love you"

Hello mommy
Hello daddy

I'm talking on the telephone to my sister, to my sister, to my sister
It's fun to talk on the telephone saying, "Sister, how are you?"

I'm talking on the telephone to my brother, to my brother, to my brother
It's fun to talk on the telephone saying, "Brother, how are you?"

Hello sister
Hello brother

I'm talking on the telephone to my grandma, to my grandma, to my grandma
It's fun to talk on the telephone saying, "Grandma, I miss you"

I'm talking on the telephone to my grandpa, to my grandpa, to my grandpa
It's fun to talk on the telephone saying, "Grandpa, I miss you"

Hello grandma
Hello grandpa

I'm talking on the telephone to my friend, to my friend, to my friend
It's fun to talk on the telephone saying, "Friend, I feel great"

I'm finished talking on the telephone now, I'm finished, I'm finished
I'm finished talking on the telephone now saying, "Friend, I've got to go"

I've got to go
I've got to go

Bye bye

Activity Signs

Telephone

Mommy

Love

I Love You

Fun

Daddy

Hello

Sister

How are You?

Brother

Grandma

I Miss You

push chin and twist

Grandpa

Friend

Hook fingers

Switch position

I Feel Great

Finished

turn hands over

I Go

Goodbye

wave goodbye to phone then hang up

Additional Sign

I Love You

47

Jumping Up and Down

Lyrics

I'm jumping up and down, jumping up and down
Just like a little frog I'm jumping up and down

I'm walking on my toes, on my tippy toes
Just like a tall giraffe I'm walking on my toes

I'm crawling on the ground, crawling on the ground
Just like a little bug I'm crawling on the ground

I'm rolling on the ground, rolling on the ground
Just like a little dog I'm rolling on the ground

I'm stomping on the ground, stomping on the ground
Just like an elephant, I'm stomping on the ground

I'm turning all around, turning all around
Just like a little child, I'm turning all around
Turning all around, turning all around
Just like a little child, I'm turning all around

All this has made me dizzy, so now I'm falling down

Activity Overview

This song will have your children jumping, walking, crawling, and rolling—just like their favorite creatures! Its complexity exposes children to a rich tapestry of overlapping rhythms, instrumentation and activity. If you want a break from signing, this song can also be a movement activity where children just pretend to be each animal.

Notes from Joseph

The sign for "Just Like," meaning "The Same," is used in a variety of contexts in ASL. If someone signs, "I'm Tired," another person may sign "Just Like," meaning me too. In this song, you can introduce the Additional Sign of "Just Like" during the phrase, "Just like a _____ ." This sign is not to be confused with the sign for "Like," as in the phrase, "I like this song." You can find the sign "Like" in the song "Let's Go Riding."

Jumping Up and Down

● Mime or movement

1st grader, Savannah, jumps high during playtime

Jump Up and Down
●

Frog
flick out fingers twice

Walk on Toes
●

Giraffe

Crawl on the Floor
●

Bug

Roll on the Floor
●

Dog
slap leg

Stomp on the Ground
●

Elephant

Twirl in a Circle
●

Child

Crouch Down (falling down)
●

Just Like

Additional Signs

Go to the Beach

Activity Overview

This upbeat song is ideal for reinforcing vocabulary that children can use during a trip to the beach. The sign sequences we suggest for this song are simplified to keep pace with its playful spirit. Our recommended sign for "Beach" is the sign for "Ocean" in ASL, because it makes for a more easily signed sequence. Signs for "splash," "dig," and "fly" kites are all iconic, meaning they look like the action they describe. Surf's up! Let's go!

Notes from Joseph

If I were interpreting the meaning of this song to a person who is deaf, I wouldn't sign the sequence, "Go, Beach, You" as we have done here. Instead, I would use the signs "Beach, You/Me, Together/Go/There." For very young signers, however, the signs suggested for "Go, Beach, You" are easier to produce and reinforce the lyrics, including the word "You," which is among kids' favorites. For additional fun and simplicity, we recommend continuing the mime action of "Digging" through the phrase, "Let's get out our pails, go looking for snails." Sometimes, simplicity is the best approach, especially with the youngest signers.

Lyrics

I want to go to the beach with you
Go to the beach with you
Havin' some fun, enjoyin' the sun
Go to the beach with you

I want to splash
In the waves with you
Splash in the waves with you
Our feet in the sea
You laughin' with me
Splash in the waves with you

I want to dig in the sand with you
Dig in the sand with you
Get out our pails
Go lookin' for snails
Dig in the sand with you

I want to go on a walk with you
Go on a walk with you
Our feet in the sand
Just holdin' your hand
Go on a walk with you

I want to go
   Just go
   Go to the beach
I want to go
   Just go
   Go to the beach
I want to go
   Just go
   Go to the beach
With you, Oooooo

I want to fly my new kite with you
Fly my new kite with you
We'll make it fly high
Right into the sky
Fly my new kite with you

I want to ride in a boat with you
Ride in a boat with you
Playin' all day, out on the waves
Ride in a boat with you

Clap your hands

I want to go to the beach with you
Go to the beach with you
Havin' some fun, enjoyin' the sun
Go to the beach with you

Havin' some fun enjoyin' the sun
I want to go to the beach with you
Havin' some fun, enjoyin' the sun
I want to go to the beach with you

Clap your hands

Ooooo
I want to go!

Go to the Beach

Tim shows his friend how to sign "You"

Go

Beach

like waves

You

Fun

touch nose, move down to fingers

Sun

Splash

Dig

Walk

Fly Kite

Boat

Additional Signs

Go There with You

With

Track 19
Let's Go Riding

Lyrics

Woo woo, woo woo, **let's go** riding **on a choo choo** train
Woo woo, woo, woo, **if you** like **it we can do it** again
Let's go riding **on a choo choo** train
Oooh, if you like **it we can do it** again

Zoom zoom, zoom zoom, **let's go** riding **in a big** airplane
Zoom zoom, zoom zoom, **if you** like **it we can do it** again
Let's go riding **in a big** airplane
Oooh, if you like **it we can do it** again

Ting ting, ting ting, **let's go** riding **on my brand new** bike
Ting ting, ting ting, **we can go really** fast **if you like**
Let's go riding **on my brand new** bike
Oooh, we can go **really** fast **if you like**

Beep beep, beep beep, **let's go** riding **on a city** bus
Beep beep, beep beep, **there'll be plenty of room for us**
Let's go riding **on a city** bus
Oooh, There'll be plenty of room for us

Honk honk, honk honk, **let's go** riding **in a little** car
Honk honk, honk honk, **we can drive it** near or far
Let's go riding **in a little** car
Oooh, we can drive it near or far

BBbbb BBbbb, BBbbb BBbbb, **let's go** riding **in a motor** boat
BBbbb BBbbb, BBbbb BBbbb, **on the water it's so fun to float**
Let's go riding **in a motor** boat
Oooh, on the water it's so fun to float

Stop **now, our** riding **is at the** end
Oooh, but if you like **it we can do it** again

Activity Overview

This song promotes vocalizations like "Woo, woo" and "Zoom, zoom," while teaching important transportation signs. Mobile toddlers and preschoolers will probably prefer a mime version so they can pretend to be a train or plane, or to drive a car while making the appropriate sounds. For pre-mobile children, we suggest that you use the signs and vocalizations presented below. In case you're wondering, we chose to sing "Ting" for our bike bell because it's easier for young children to pronounce than "Ring." Fasten your seat belts and "Let's Go Riding!"

Notes from Joseph

"Near" and "Far" have separate signs in ASL. However, the idea of traveling near or far can be built into the "Drive" sign. "Near" and "Far" have various signs in ASL depending on the sentence context. For this song, the signers holding the "steering wheel" would move their hands away from their bodies a short distance to mean "Near" and further away from their bodies to show "Far." Slowing down the movement and adding a labored expression will convey the long distance.

Activity Signs

Mime or movement

Woo Woo

Ride

Train

Like
touch chest, pull out

Again

Airplane
like flying a plane

Ring Bell **(ting ting)**

Bike

Honk Bus Horn

Bus

Honk Car Horn **(honk honk)**

Car

Near or Far

Boat

Stop

Finished

Additional Signs

Big

Little

Room for Us

Track 20
Sleepy Time is Near

Lyrics

Where is baby's pillow?
Where oh tell me where?
Here is baby's pillow
Sleepy time is near

Where is baby's blanket?
Where oh tell me where?
Here is baby's blanket
Sleepy time is near

Lay your head right down, close your little eyes
Listen to the sound of a sleepy lullaby

Where is baby's Teddy?
Where oh tell me where?
Here is baby's Teddy
Sleepy time is near

Where is baby's hug?
Where oh tell me where?
Here is baby's hug
Sleepy time is near

Lay your head right down, close your little eyes
Listen to the sound of a sleepy lullaby

Where are baby's dreams?
Where oh tell me where?
Here come baby's dreams
Sleepy time is here

Activity Overview

Imagine a bedtime ritual where each crib item is accounted for: baby's pillow, blanket, and teddy bear—all wrapped up in a great big hug! Dim the lights, put on the Pick Me Up! CD, and sign the items in the song as you help gather them. This song is extra long to facilitate your child's transition to slumber, and can be particularly useful becaaaaaaaawwn. Zzzzzzzz.

Notes from Joseph

The sign "Bed" is used instead of "Sleepy" because the "Bed" sign is more iconic, closely resembling the child's position while sleeping.
If a baby prefers a cuddly item other than a teddy bear, use a descriptive sign like "Tiger" or "Dog," or find an appropriate sign specifically for that item. Don't forget to reinforce the signs in this song at each sleepy time and during any daily activities when these signs might be appropriate.

Activity Signs
Sleepy Time is Near

● Mime or movement

Where
finger moves, side to side

Baby

Pillow

Show Pillow

Bed (sleep)

Blanket

Show Blanket

Head Down

Close Eyes

Hear

Music (lullaby)

Bear
like claws scratching

Show Teddy Bear

Hug

Hug Baby

Dreams

More… *Karaoke Style*

Activity Overview

This song is the same song as "More Milk" (Track 4), except the recorded vocals are silent where they would normally sing the food or drink. Now, you can sing and sign items of your own choosing. There are two ways to use this song in a class environment. First, decide in advance which foods (or nouns) you and your class will sign, write them down and refer to them as you lead the activity. The second approach is more interactive. While singing and signing the song, your children take turns (in order around the circle) deciding which sign everyone will perform for the next verse. So the person whose turn it is signs and sings their choice first at the top of the verse, then everyone else joins in. The beauty in this is that children will sometimes choose nonsensical items, like "More Frog." What fun!

Notes from Joseph

Only if there are items for which you can simply find no ASL signs, create your own "homemade signs". Make the movement as iconic as possible, mimicking the shape of the item or the manner in which you interact with it. For many reasons however, it is important to use the actual ASL sign, if one exists!

Lyrics

More… _____

More… _____

Please **may I have** more… _____ ?

More… _____

More… _____

Please **may I have** more… _____ ?

For mine's all gone,

I want more… _____

REPEAT

More… *Karaoke Style*

Carrots — twist wrist, mime eating carrot

Ice Cream — mime licking ice cream

Meat — pinch meaty part of your hand

Noodles — like a wiggly noodle

"O's" (O-shaped cereal)

Pear

Pizza — "P" hand shape draws the letter "Z"

Popcorn

Additional Signs

More

Please

Want

All-Gone

Cookie(s)

Index of Signs

More from SIGN2ME®
Signing Resources to Empower Early Learning

Sign2Me is the first company in the world to introduce a true-to-ASL Signs baby signing program!

SIGN *with your* BABY®

$49⁹⁵ msrp

The Complete Learning Kit (DVD or VHS) (for all children 6 months and older)

Learn Baby Signing from the most award-winning program of its kind. When introducing American Sign Language (ASL) signs to all children, this powerful package can help you understand and meet the needs of the infants and toddlers in your care long before they can speak. Teachers and parents alike find its Book, DVD/Video, and Quick Reference Guide fun and easy to understand. Author and researcher, Dr. Joseph Garcia, offers a straightforward and light-hearted approach to teaching infants how to communicate using simple ASL signs. Joseph and the SIGN *with your* BABY® method have been featured regularly in the national media, including ABC's *20/20, Discovery Health Channel, Parent Magazine, The New York Times* and more…

SIGN *with your* BABY®

The Book

Dr. Joseph Garcia uses anecdotes, practical guidelines and humor to engage the reader. The book is easily read in two, half-hour sessions. 145 signs, along with helpful advice, and clearly-illustrated signs make this a useful reference, enabling you to quickly open this exciting link of communication with your baby!

$14⁹⁵ msrp

SIGN *with your* BABY®

The Training Video (DVD or VHS)

Winner of six national awards, this 63 minute video makes learning easy with instruction, demonstrations of 145 signs, and tips from author, Dr. Joseph Garcia. It also features practical insight from Dr. Burton White, a leading authority on early childhood development. Eye-opening footage of signing babies, along with parent testimonials offer an inspirational vision of the power of the SIGN *with your* BABY® method.

$29⁹⁵ msrp

SIGN *with your* BABY®

The Quick Reference Guide

This attractive, laminated reference tool illustrates 54 of the most useful signs and can help you monitor each child's signing progress. Get one for each infant and toddler in your care to show parents and other caregivers the signs a baby knows and uses, and to have a fun keepsake for this important developmental stage.

$9⁹⁵ msrp

ASL Flash Cards Packs

These durable ASL-based flash cards are designed to make it fun for everyone to expand their signing vocabulary. The front of each card displays a colorful illustration while the reverse side teaches you how to make the associated sign. Each card displays English, Spanish and ASL.

Quick Start Pack *Includes:* Eat • Milk • More • Mommy • and many more...

Animals & Colors Pack *Includes:* Dog • Bird • Purple • Green • and many more...

Family, Clothing, & Toileting Pack *Includes:* Friend • Grandpa • Baby • Change • and many more...

Objects & Emotions Pack *Includes:* Happy • Hungry • Airplane • Car • and many more...

Actions & Opposites Pack *Includes:* Dance • Little • Rain • Stars • and many more...

$**11**^95 **ea.**
msrp

Linda Stoler Music CDs

$**14**^95 **ea.**
msrp

As parents and educators listen and sing along with these music CD's, children will naturally be drawn to your face and the movements of your mouth. At other times, when a child is being soothed by the music, she/he will respond to specific, recognizable sound patterns. When infants and young children are exposed to language in an interactive manner, they learn to make order from what they hear. As you and your child share the experience of these songs, your relationship deepens and your child's knowledge and sense of self expands. Enjoy often for best results! Hear samples of Linda's engaging music at www.sign2me.com

Pick Me Up! ASL Nursery Rhyme Posters Set

These ASL-based posters include your favorite traditional nursery rhyme lyrics with matching sign illustrations and descriptions, American Sign Language tips, and related activities. The **Pick Me Up! Nursery Rhyme Poster** Set of eight include: "The Alphabet Song," "Little Boy Blue," "Humpty Dumpty," "Little Miss Muffet," "Jack & Jill," "One, Two, Buckle My Shoe," "This Little Piggy," and "Hey Diddle Diddle."

$**39**^95
msrp

Receive **3 FREE Gifts** when you subscribe to the FREE Sign2Me *Spotlight Newsletter*

FREE MP3
Song from the award winning Pick Me Up! Music CD

6 FREE
Getting started signs to get started signing today!

ASL
Alphabet signs chart!

The Sign2Me Spotlight Newsletter features educational and insightful articles and stories from our diverse Instructors' Network. Get useful ASL (American Sign Language) sign demonstrations, information about early literacy, seasonal discounts and much, much More! If you're looking to join fun classes to learn and share signing experience with other families, we offer that too, taught by over 700 Certified Sign2Me Instructors. Sign2Me is the world leader and the first company ever to develop and offer a true-to-ASL Sign Language, Baby Sign Language program.

Subscribe to our FREE Spotlight Newsletter online at:

Sign2Me Online

www. SIGN2ME® .com

SIGN2ME®

12125 Harbour Reach Dr. Suite D
Mukilteo, WA 98275

SIGN2ME®

Registration Card

Please take a few moments to fill out this registration card and receive additional FREE benefits.

Name:_____

Address:_____

City:_____State:_____Zip:_____

Email:_____

❑   I am a teacher or Childcare Provider.

❑   I'd like a FREE subscription to the *Spotlight Newsletter* where I will get insightful stories
and tips from Sign2Me signing parents and Instructors as well as other discounts and specials.

Comments:_____
_____
_____
_____